The Bride's Pocket Guide to
Wedding Customs & Superstitions

The Bride's Pocket Guide to Wedding Customs & Superstitions

By
Christina Cerullo

The Dark Ages of New England Books
www.DarkAgesofNewEngland.com

The Bride's Pocket Guide to Wedding Customs
and Superstitions
by Christina Cerullo
Copyright © 2011 published by Sinematix

First Edition

The Bride's Pocket Guide to Wedding Customs
and Superstitions
Copyright © 2011 Sinematix
ISBN 978-1-257-85456-1

Sinematix
P.O. Box 841
Brookfield, CT 06804

www.DarkAgesofNewEngland.com

Table of Contents

Introduction

Modern weddings are filled with traditions dating back to the dawn of written history. Many of these traditions and customs are still being practiced today, but what is the meaning behind them? From the engagement to the honeymoon, brides and grooms continue to follow these very precise rituals without even knowing why.

As generations have come and gone, many of these traditions have lost their original meanings, but many still believe that these credulous, irrational beliefs must be done or the marriage will fail! The histories behind many of these superstitions are quite interesting and almost unbelievable. Nowadays the bride is the center of attention and the princess for the day, but at one time it was completely the opposite.

As with all superstitions, they are only as real as you make them, the only real rule to follow is to relax and enjoy your wedding. Although, it wouldn't hurt to keep this guide close by, just in case...

The Engagement

Customs

The Engagement Ring

In olden times a groom would purchase his bride from her family with precious gems, land, or livestock as a promise of marriage. Modern brides are no longer paid for, but a gift is still given, usually in the form of an engagement ring.

A diamond is the most common stone used in an engagement ring. The fire of the diamond is considered a symbol of how much the husband-to-be loves his bride; the brighter the fire the more he loves her. Opals, pearls, and emeralds are all considered unlucky for engagement rings, while rubies, sapphires, and turquoise are thought to be lucky. Any blue or Tiger's Eye stones are said to protect the bride from evil, witchcraft and ward off the evil eye.

The Engagement Party

This party for the couple's families to formally meet each other is traditionally hosted by the bride's family. These celebrations began during ancient Greece and were used by the groom and the bride's father to form an official oral contract for the marriage to take place. Often in these times the bride did not attend her own engagement party.

Superstitions

~ It is bad luck for the bride-to-be to remove her engagement ring. If she does, it must be replaced by the one that gave it to her.

~ It is considered bad luck for another woman to try on your engagement ring, because she will be the woman that steals her fiancée. Contrary in Scottish tradition, a woman can try on an engagement ring for good luck and should spin the ring three times towards their heart to attract love to her.

~ The wedding band should never be purchased at the same time as the engagement ring, it is bad luck.

~ The wedding band should never be worn before the wedding or the marriage will be doomed.

~ It is good luck for the bride to dream of her wedding day, even if the dream is negative.

~ It is bad luck for the bride and groom to share their birthdays within the same month and it is even worse if they share the same birthday.

~ A bride should never practice writing her new name before the wedding, it will bring bad luck.

~ It is bad luck to marry a man whose last name starts with the same letter as the brides. There is even the rhyme:

> To change the name and not the letter,
> Is to change for the worse and not the better.

The Bridal Shower

Customs

The earliest bridal shower-like traditions can be traced back to the Netherlands in the 16th and 17th centuries. During this time, Americans started a similar practice of making a "hope chest" for the bride-to-be. A hope chest (also known as a dowry chest) was used by the young woman and her family to collect all the items needed for her future marriage. The first documented actual "bridal showers" were in Brussels, Belgium around the 1860's. This custom reached America in the 1890's and became widespread by the 1930's.

A bridal shower originally was for poor women or for those whose father refused to pay her dowry because he did not approve of her future husband. The bride-to-be's friends and family would gather together and shower her with gifts to compensate for the absence of her dowry, so she would have everything needed for her new home and family.

Medieval England had their own type of bridal shower to raise money for the bride. The day before the wedding during the pre-wedding feast, the bride would sell bruydale or "Bride Ale," which she made both for the wedding celebration and to fund her dowry. This special beer was made with very high quality ingredients compared to their everyday beer.

Ribbons

Ribbons are a symbol of fertility at bridal showers. For every ribbon broken by the bride while opening her gifts at a bridal shower, she will have a child.

The Bow-quet

It is customary for the bride to keep the ribbons and bows from the presents received at the bridal shower to make a make-shift ribbon bouquet called a *bow-quet*. They are usually arranged on a paper plate to create a faux bouquet that is used at the rehearsal dinner for good luck. Sometimes the leftover ribbons and bows not used in the *bow-quet* are used to make a faux veil which is used for the same reason.

Superstitions

~ It is bad luck to receive cutlery or sharp objects as a gift, so do not register for them. Buy them after the wedding.

~ The first gift the bride opens at her shower should be the first one used.

~ The gift giver of the third gift opened will be the next to have a baby.

~ If the bride receives a wooden spoon she will be blessed with cooking skills.

~ The bride-to-be's comments should be written down as she opens her gifts, because those are the same comments she will make on her wedding night.

The Wedding Party

The Bride
Customs

Everyone has heard the rhyme: *Something old, something new, something borrowed, something blue, and a lucky six pence in her shoe*, but few know there are specific meanings to each line. It is difficult to trace this poem back to its origins. Some believe it started during Victorian times, while others believe it dates back much older than that.

Something Old: Looks at the past, referring to the couples friends and family. Wearing something old symbolizes that her family will always be a part of her life.

Something New: Looks towards the future for health, fortune, happiness, and the couple's new union together.

Something Borrowed: Is a gift to the bride, usually from her mother, to show their love and support. Even though it might be a gift, it must be returned to its original owner for it to bring good luck. Shoes and handkerchiefs are normal items that can be borrowed and are considered extra good luck. The item borrowed should not be from a widow or a woman with an unhappy marriage because that bad luck will be carried onto the new bride.

<u>Something Blue</u>: The color blue represents fidelity heaven, spirituality, and virginity. The color blue is also used to protect the bride from evil and witches.

<u>Six Spence in Her Shoe</u>: Is to bring financial security to the couple. Some brides now use a penny instead of a six pence piece, and tape it inside their left shoe for financial luck.

Pearls

There are contradicting superstitions about brides wearing pearls. Some believe that a bride should wear pearls to ensure that she will not cry during her marriage. The opposite is believed in Mexico where the bride should not wear pearls because those are the future tears she will shed during her marriage.

Signs of Virginity

Some common virginity symbols used by a bride are: down styled hair, flowers in the hair, orange blossoms, or a wreath of flowers around the head. White wedding dresses are now considered a sign of virginity, but blue was the original color to symbolize virginity.

<u>Veil</u>

The veil originally was used to express a bride's modesty or innocence and to disguise the bride from evil on her wedding day. This was introduced by the Romans, where their brides were completely covered from head to toe in cloth. This Roman bridal outfit was worn once again as her burial shroud. Veils are also used in some cultures that have arranged marriages because the bride and groom often have never met, and the veil gives the groom no chance to back out of the arrangement if she is unattractive.

Superstitions

~ If the bride's veil is accidentally torn during the wedding (especially at the altar) it is good luck.

~ The veil should never be tried on with the dress, it is bad luck.

~ It is good luck and will bring fertility to the new bride if she borrows a veil from a happily married woman.

~ The bride should not look in a mirror completely dressed in her entire bridal outfit before the ceremony, it is bad luck. Always leave off a piece of jewelry until you are ready to walk down the aisle.

~ It is bad luck for the bride to eat while she is getting dressed for the wedding.

~ A bride should wear old shoes or borrow shoes for her wedding for good luck, and should not buy a new pair.

~ If the bride loses her garter before the ceremony, her husband will be unfaithful.

The Dress
Customs

The wedding dress was a symbol of the bride's family's affluence in the community. Marriages were often not just a union between the bride and groom; it was bonding the two families often for business purposes.

A wealthy bride wore bright colors made of extravagant imported fabrics including silks and furs, while a poor bride simply wore her best church dress. The color green was always avoided, not because it was unlucky, but because it was considered the color of promiscuity. Green was an unfaithful color because they believed that it symbolized grass stains or stains from "rolling in the hay" with men. The most common color of a wedding dress was actually blue, which was considered the color of virginity and purity, until white became more popular. The poem on the next page explains the meaning for each color of a brides dress.

Married in White, you have chosen right,
Married in Gray, sadness will come your way,
Married in Black, better turn back,
Married in Red, you will wish yourself dead,
Married in Green, ashamed to be seen,
Married in Blue, you're man will be true,
Married in Pearl, you will live in a whirl,
Married in Yellow, not marrying the right fellow,
Married in Brown, you will live in the town,
Married in Pink, your spirit will sink.

Most modern people believe that the bride wears a white dress to symbolize virginity and purity, but that is not the origin of the white dress. One reason it started is because the cloth needed to be bleached numerous times to become bright white, and the process was very expensive. Brides were originally measured by the whiteness of their dress, the whiter the dress the more affluent the bride's family.

The first princess to wear the color white instead of the traditional royal wedding color of silver was Philippa of England. White dresses became popular amongst the public when Queen Victoria copied Philippa in her marriage to Albert of Saxe-Coburg in 1840 with a widely publicized wedding portrait. Soon European brides started to copy this royal trend.

The type of material used for a bridal dress is very important when it comes to luck.

Traditional wedding dresses were silk, which was considered good luck. Dresses that are made of satin are bad luck. A dress should never be made of velvet because not only is it bad luck, it means the couple will be impoverished. The dress's material should never have a pattern on the fabric especially one with birds, which is very bad luck.

Superstitions

~ For a happy bride, she should carry a bit of salt on her wedding day. This is also to protect her from bad luck, witches, evil spirits, and the evil eye.

~ If the dress is borrowed from someone else, it will bring good luck to the new bride, but bad luck to the lender. The only exception is that if the dress is borrowed from the bride's mother, it is very good luck for both of them.

~ A wedding dress should not be used if it was bought for another wedding. The new marriage will be cursed like the first wedding that did not take place.

~ The final stitch of the dress should not be completed until leaving for the wedding, otherwise it is bad luck.

~ A bride should never make her own wedding dress, it brings very bad luck.

~ The entire bridal outfit should never be tried on before the wedding day, it is considered bad luck.

~ If your dress is ripped during the wedding it means the marriage will end in death.

~ If the bridal dress becomes stained with blood from the bride or anyone else, it is a very bad omen.

~ If the bride spills something red on her dress like wine, she has not been honest with her husband about her sexual history.

~ It is good luck to find a spider in your wedding gown.

~ Another good luck charm is that the bride should sew a few of her own hairs into her dress.

Bride Maids and the Maid of Honor
Customs

Bride Maids are thought to originate from an old Roman law that required ten witnesses for the wedding ceremony to be legal. They were dressed in very similar outfits to the bride, in attempt to protect the bride from evil spirits and ill wishes. They were also used to distract men from knowing which woman was actually the bride from bride kidnappers. Now bridesmaids primarily help the bride plan and get ready for her wedding.

The original term "maid of honor" is the title given to a Queen's attendant. This title was granted to the most honored bridesmaid because the bride is considered the queen for the day and she is her attendant. If a "maid of honor" is married then the title "matron of honor" is used instead. The maid of honor is the maid that stands closest to the bride during the ceremony and often helps with the preparation and planning of the wedding. She also assists the bride all wedding day and usually holds the brides bouquet during the ceremony. If the bridesmaid is between the 8 and 15 years of age they are called a junior bridesmaid.

There are conflicting superstitions of whether bridesmaids and groomsmen with red hair are considered lucky or unlucky. In gypsy lore they are very good luck. In the United Kingdom and United States they are unlucky, are thought to be bad tempered and should not be trusted. People during medieval times believed those with fire red hair were witches and even worked with the Devil, and therefore should never be trusted and were often killed.

Superstitions

~ There are two similar sayings about bridesmaids; "Twice a bridesmaid, never a bride" or "Three times a bridesmaid, never a bride."

The Groom
Customs

Bachelor or stag parties

This tradition actually goes back to the 5th century with the Spartans. It originally was a bachelor's dinner where all the family and friends gathered the evening before the wedding to eat and drink in the grooms honor, as a farewell dinner. Now most bachelor parties are done farther from the wedding date because rehearsal dinners are done the night before. Bachelor parties now are often wilder than the original farewell dinner and often have female entertainers, but it did not start that way.

Tuxedo

The tuxedo outfit that almost every groom wears for his wedding suit originated back in 1860. Henry Poole & Company based out of London, England created a short tail-less black smoking jacket for the Prince of Wales (who later became King Edward VII), which was meant to be worn at informal dinners as a lounging suit. In 1886 it was introduced into the United States by a New Yorker named James Potter. He went to Henry Poole & Co. to buy his new dinner suit for a party at the Tuxedo Park Club, and purchased one of the smoking jackets. This outfit became all the rage and everyone in the Tuxedo Park Club began to dress in this new style, and is where the name "tuxedo" came from for this ensemble. Tuxedos are traditionally worn by the groom, groomsmen, the bride's father, and often the ring bearer.

Superstitions

~ If the groom drops the wedding ring during the ceremony, their marriage will fail.

~ A groom traditionally wore the color gray instead of black because it was a color of mourning and bad luck.

~ It is bad luck for someone to congratulate the bride directly; it should always be said to the groom instead.

~ During Victorian times they believed that it was good luck to be married the same week of the groom's birthday. It was especially good luck if they married on his birthday.

~ It's good luck for the groom to wear a shirt given to him by his fiancée for the wedding.

~ It is an Italian custom for the groom to carry a piece of iron in his pocket to keep away the evil eye. Iron is a metal that is known to detour and banish evil.

~ The groom should carry a miniature horseshoe in his pocket for good luck.

~ The groom should wear a miniature version of the bridal bouquet as a boutonniere. This comes from the medieval tradition where a knight would wear his lady's colors to show his love and devotion to her.

~ A groom is not supposed to see his bride before the ceremony on the wedding day; it is considered back luck and means the marriage will fail.

Groomsmen and the Best Man
Customs

Originally groomsmen or "bride-knights" were used to help the groom capture or abduct the groom's bride if there was resistance. If the bride or bride's family did not approve of the groom, the groom and groomsmen abducted her and she was forced into the marriage. Bride kidnapping was common in early societies including the New England area in the United States, and is unfortunately still practiced in different parts of the world today. Some churches even had a hidden vault beneath the altar where weapons were hidden like knives, spears, or swords in case the groom and the groomsmen needed to fend off the bride's family.

The best man primarily had two responsibilities. One to prevent the bride from running away or being taken back by her family, and the second was to protect the rings until the ceremony. The best man and groomsmen roles eventually became similar to the bridesmaid role were they protected the groom from evil. The best man and groomsmen also wear almost identical outfits to the groom so that demons cannot identify and attack the groom.

In colonial New England groomsmen were also used for another tradition in the Connecticut area. According to the journal of Madam Sarah Kemble Knights written in 1704, when a groom would get cold feet before the wedding, the groomsmen would literally drag him back to his duty. So whether the groomsmen were forcing a bride into marriage or making sure the groom fulfilled his bridegroom duties, they were the enforcers of the ceremony.

The Flower Girl

The flower girl custom started during Ancient Greece and Rome but instead of flowers, the young girl would carry sheaths of wheat and herbs. She would scatter them on the ground before the bride, symbolizing and wishing the bride fertility and prosperity. By the medieval era, flower girls still carried sheaths of wheat for fertility, but also carried strong smelling garlic and herbs to ward off evil spirits. Each of the different herbs had specific meanings depending upon the type. For the descriptions of herb and flower meanings, see *The Ceremony* section starting on page 33.

In Elizabethan times the flower girl would come out following the musicians, spreading flowers all the way from the bride's home to the church and often carried a bride's cup. A bride cup was often made out of silver and carried gilded rosemary twigs that were tied together with colorful ribbons or "bride laces." These were given to the wedding guests as gifts and were used to dip in their sack-posset or wine. During the Victorian and Edwardian eras, flower girls wore white dresses with colored sashes which are still common today.

Modern flower girls normally are the last person to walk down the aisle before the bride with a basket of flower petals. Generally flower girls are between the ages of 3 and 8, and if over 8 years of age they are considered a junior bridesmaid, but technically there are no age restrictions. She throws the petals (usually roses) onto the ground to prevent the evil spirits from hell from attacking the bride. Depending upon the color of the rose petal each has a different meaning; <u>Blue</u>: hope, <u>Green</u>: youth, <u>Orange</u>: vitality, <u>Pink</u>: sweetness, <u>Red</u>: love, and <u>White</u>: purity and innocence. In the United Kingdom flower girls commonly throw yellow rose petals to ensure fertility for the bride.

The Ring Bearer and Coinbearer

The origin of ring bearer is not exactly known. Some believe it dates back as far as Ancient Egypt, but they did not become common until the Victorian era. During medieval times instead of having a ring bearer the ring was presented to the bride on the tip of a sword as a symbol of its importance.

The ring pillow carried by the ring bearer comes from a king and queen coronation ceremony, where the crown is carried on a pillow to those being coronated. This practice was adopted into weddings where the rings were carried like a royal crown because the bride and groom are considered royalty for the day. The ring bearer traditionally wore a white lace collar and sash, but now they wear a suit or a miniature matching tuxedo to groom and groomsmen.

A coinbearer's role is similar to the ring bearer but carries wedding coins or "wedding arrhae" down the aisle. The coins are usually thirteen gold and silver coins used to represent Jesus and the Apostles and are given to the clergyman as a blessing. The role of the coinbearer is not common anymore especially since silver and gold coins are no longer made.

The Wedding Day

Customs

The days of the week and months all have different meanings for wedding dates according to their old rhymes. Weddings traditionally did not take place on Sundays so that day is omitted from the rhyme.

<u>Days</u>

> Monday for health,
> Tuesday for wealth,
> Wednesday best of all,
> Thursday for losses,
> Friday for crosses,
> Saturday for no luck at all.

<u>Months</u>

Married when the year is new, He'll be loving, kind and true,

When *February* birds do mate, You wed nor dread your fate,

If you wed when *March* winds blow, Joy and sorrow both you'll know,

Marry in *April* when you can, Joy for Maiden and for Man,

Marry in the month of *May*, and you'll surely rue the day,

Marry when *June* roses grow, Over land and sea you'll go,

Those who in *July* do wed, Must labor for their daily bread,

Whoever wed in *August* be, Many a change is sure to see,

Marry in *September's* shrine, Your living will be rich and fine,

If in *October* you do marry, Love will come but riches tarry,

If you wed in bleak *November*, Only joys will come, remember,

When *December* snows fall fast, Marry and true love will last.

Marry in Lent, Live to repent.

It is considered very bad luck to marry during Lent. The unluckiest month in almost every country, not just the United States, is the month of May. Many societies consider it unlucky because the Feast of the Dead is during May and therefore there is no room for a celebration of the living. People believe that if a couple gets married during May, they will be childless or their children will be cursed with health issues and physical deformities.

Superstitions
<u>Weather</u>

Who wants it to rain on their wedding day? Well actually you should want it to rain; it is considered very good luck. It is said for every drop of rain that falls on your wedding day that is one less tear you will shed during your marriage. Others believe that the rain is tears from previous boyfriends and lovers crying over the loss of the bride to another man. It is also a symbol of fertility, the more it rains, the more children the couple will be blessed with.

If the skies are overcast and windy, the marriage will be stormy. If it is snowing, that implies the newlyweds will be showered with wealth and fertility during their marriage.

Despite the promise of rain bringing good luck and fertility, brides throughout the ages have come up with many different methods to stop the rain. Here are a few:

~ Place a statue of the Virgin Mary on a window sill in your home.

~ Hang rosary beads in a window or outside your home the day of your wedding.

~ Boil rocks in a pot of water on your wedding day.

~ Feed your cat the morning of the wedding just before you leave.

Good Luck Omens

It is considered good luck for a bride to see or encounter these on the way to her wedding: a chimney sweep, dove, frog, toad, black cat, lamb, or rainbow. Some brides went as far as to hire a chimney sweep on their wedding day to ensure good luck. It is especially good luck if the chimney sweep kisses the bride on her cheek.

It is good luck for a groom to see or encounter: a pigeon, wolf, or a nanny goat on the way to the ceremony. The groom should also give a coin to the first person he meets that day for good luck.

Bad Luck Omens

It is considered bad luck if you see or encounter these on the way to your wedding: pig, hare, dog, owl, serpent, funeral procession, an open grave, blind man, pregnant woman, if a lizard crosses your path, or if you hear a rooster crow after dawn. If a bride is unlucky enough to meet a nun or monk on the way to the wedding, she will be cursed with barrenness and will never have children. It is also bad luck for two brides to meet on their way to their weddings.

The Ceremony

Customs

The custom of giving away the bride traditionally is done by her father, and is a relic from when women were considered property. With this act he literally hands over ownership of his daughter to her new husband. Nowadays the father giving away the bride is considered a blessing by the parents of the bride, and shows approval of the marriage.

The bride takes her father's right arm and is escorted down the aisle, where she is handed off to the groom, and takes her place to the groom's left. This customary position started because it was easier for the groom to draw his sword on his right side to defend his bride from rival suitors, or the bride's family from stopping the ceremony if she was a kidnapped bride.

Rice

People began throwing rice at weddings to wish the newly married couple fertility, luck, happiness, and prosperity. Traditionally the guests threw rice over the newlyweds after the ceremony and would cheer, "Bread for life and pudding forever," to wish them affluence. Wheat grains were also thrown, but were not used as commonly as rice.

The Receiving Line

Directly following the ceremony the newlyweds are considered to be good luck so everyone attending the ceremony takes turns touching the couple wishing them well, and hoping it will be passed onto them.

The Kiss

The kiss at the end of the ceremony began during Roman times because a kiss sealed a deal or contract, and was as legally binding as a signature. It is still done for the same reason and also represents the bride and groom exchanging their souls to one another and becoming one.

Superstitions

~ If a candle lit on your wedding day is extinguished by an unseen hand; it is a warning that evil spirits are nearby.

~ There should be no mirrors in the ceremony area, it is bad luck.

~ If the bride or groom drops a wedding ring during the ceremony, they will be the first to die.

~ If the ring is dropped in a church and rolls onto a gravestone, depending upon if the deceased is a man or a woman the spouse of that sex will be the first to die.

~ A wedding band is worn on the left index finger because they believed the vein from that finger goes directly to the heart.

~ The rings should be blessed by a clergyman or priest for good health and to ward off demons and evil.

~ A wedding band must fit correctly because if it is too loose, the marriage will not stay together and if the band is too tight the marriage will be full of jealousy.

~ It is a widespread belief that if the second hand on a clock is going up when the ceremony ends it is good luck.

~ The bride should enter the church with her left foot first for good luck.

~ It is bad luck to start walking down the aisle on time.

~ It is bad luck for the bride to come down the aisle to The Wedding March (*Here Comes the Bride*). It is from an opera where the bride betrays her husband, so he leaves her and she dies.

~ To ensure fertility, the bride should kiss a baby's head on her wedding day.

~ If the ceremony is done in a church, the bells must ring loudly while the new couple is leaving the church to protect them from evil spirits.

~ It is good luck to have a bat in the church during the ceremony.

The Flowers

Depending upon the region of the world, there were different flower customs for each area. In early Greece the bride and groom both wore a garland around their neck made of pungent herbs and spices. Celtic people did the same, but added thistle, ivy, and heather which now are symbols of Celtic nationality.

Bouquets can be traced back to ancient times, but was originally made of garlic, aromatic herbs and spices instead of flowers. This was done thinking that the strong smelling ingredients would ward off evil spirits. Also the herbs helped hide the bride's body odor because people during these times did not practice good hygiene to say the least, and wouldn't bathe often. Dill the herb of lust, was always in the bouquet and was eaten by the bride and groom to increase their sexual desires and increase their chances of conceiving a child. A "kissing knot" was made of rosemary, ribbons, and leaves and was hung above the couple at their wedding feast to inspire loyalty. On the next page is a list of herbs and their meanings.

Bouquet Herb Meanings

Allspice: Compassion
Basil: Love and hope
Bay Leaf: Strength
Coriander: Lust
Dill: Lust
Garlic: Courage, strength, and to ward off evil.
Juniper: Protection
Mint: Protection from illness
Marjoram: Joy
Rosemary: Remembrance and loyalty
Sage: Wisdom
Thyme: Strength and courage
Wheat: Fertility

The practice of using flowers in bouquets became frequent during Victorian times. Victorians developed a language of flowers called *floriography*, where the different types of flowers and colors had specific meanings. This language was able to express feelings and love without even saying a spoken or written word. Most Victorians still used some aromatic herbs and spices in the bouquet alongside the flowers.

Modern brides now pick flowers solely because of the season they are being married, cost, and color scheme to their wedding. The following list has some of the most common wedding flowers and their floriography meanings.

Flower Meanings

Azaleas: Temperance

Baby's Breath: Innocence and everlasting love

Bachelor Button: Celibacy

Bittersweet: Truth

Carnation: Affection. (<u>Pink</u>: friendship, <u>Purple</u>: whimsical, <u>Red</u>: love, <u>White</u>: innocence and purity, <u>Yellow</u>: rejection)

Chrysanthemum: Cheerfulness and wealth (<u>Red</u>: love, <u>White</u>: truth, <u>Yellow</u>: slighted love)

Cornflower: Hope and admiration

Crocus: Cheerfulness

Cyclamen: Resignation

Daffodil: Respect

Daisy (Gerbera): Innocence or purity

Delphinium: An open heart and love

Forget-Me-Not: True love and memories

Foxglove: Insincerity

Freesia: Trust

Gladiolus: Love at first sight

Heather: (<u>Purple</u>: admiration, <u>White</u>: protection)

Hibiscus: Beauty

Holly: Good will

Honeysuckle: Devoted affection

Hyacinth: Rashness (<u>Blue</u>: constancy, <u>Purple</u>: sorrow, <u>Red or pink</u>: playfulness, <u>White</u>: loveliness, <u>Yellow</u>: jealousy)

Hydrangea: Understanding and heartlessness

Iris: Wisdom and communication

Ivy: Fidelity and friendship

Larkspur: Infidelity (<u>Pink</u>: fickleness)

Lavender: Distrust or devotion

Lilac: Purity and innocence

Lilies: Protection from evil. (<u>Calla</u>: beauty, <u>Orange</u>: hatred, <u>Tiger</u>: wealth, <u>Stargazer</u>: wealth, <u>White</u>: virginity and purity, <u>Yellow</u>: falseness)

Lily of the Valley: Happiness. This flower is a popular choice for remarrying widows.

Magnolia: Sweetness. This flower is a popular choice amongst southern brides.

Mistletoe: Affection

Orange Blossom: Virginity, purity, chastity, and loveliness. These were commonly used in Victorian wedding bouquets and in the bride's hair.

Orchid: Beauty and love

Pansy: Thought

Peony: Determination and shame

Poppy: Imagination and pleasure

Rhododendron: Fascination

Rose: Love (<u>Black</u>: death, <u>Coral</u>: desire, <u>Peach</u>: admiration and gratitude, <u>Pink</u>: happiness, <u>Red</u>: true love and courage, <u>Deep Red</u>: beauty and passion, <u>Orange</u>: fascination, <u>Purple</u>: uniqueness and enchantment, <u>White</u>: innocence, eternal love, and humility, <u>Yellow</u>: friendship or jealousy). It is bad luck to have red roses in the bridal bouquet; the marriage will end in death.

Rose bud: Beauty, youth, and innocence. (<u>Red</u>: purity and beauty, <u>White</u>: young women and innocent love)

Salvia: Thoughtfulness

Stephanotis: Happiness in marriage

Sunflower: Loyalty

Sweet Pea: Pleasure

Tulip: Passion (<u>Red</u>: love, <u>Yellow</u>: hopeless love)

Veronica: Fidelity

Violet: Modesty and faithfulness (<u>Blue</u>: love)

     The color combination of just red and white flowers in the bridal bouquet should be avoided because it represents blood and bandages.

The Reception

Customs

The First Dance

This first dance signifies the opening of the reception and originally was done for the groom to show off his new bride.

Bouquet Toss

It is customary for the bride to throw a bouquet (often not her real bouquet) over her shoulder behind her to a group of single women, which often leads to crazed frenzy to catch it. The woman that catches the bouquet is supposed to be the next to marry. Before the tradition of the bouquet being thrown, an old shoe was used instead, but had the same meaning.

Garter Belt

There are two different theories to the origin of throwing the garter belt. The first story is that it was customary for a witness to be present in the bedroom to confirm that consummation of the marriage was completed. Eventually this practice was considered a violation of privacy so the husband would take off the wife's garter belt and throw it to a witness outside the bedroom to signal completion of the act.

The second version is that it started during the 14th century with the belief that it is good luck to have a piece of the newlyweds clothing. During this time it was not uncommon for people to tear the brides dress to get a piece for good luck, so they started throwing the garter belt to distract people away from the bride.

In colonial New England they did throw the garter belt, but it had a twist. Often the bridesmaids and unmarried girls would try to steal the garter by craftiness or trickery away from the man that caught it. They believed this would give them good luck and they soon would be married.

The throwing of the garter belt is still done at many weddings to this day. Now the groom is supposed to remove the garter belt from the brides thigh (usually with his teeth, but that is optional) and throws it over his shoulder behind his back to the single men. Whoever catches the garter belt is the next one to marry. The man that catches the garter belt is then supposed to place it on the leg of the woman that caught the bouquet. I have witnessed and heard of a few instances where a very young girl caught the bouquet, so instead of having the man place the garter on the underage girl's leg, the opposite is done where she would place it on his leg.

<u>Clanking glasses</u>

During the reception people would clank their glasses thinking the sound would repel the devil and evil spirits away giving the bride and groom a safe time to kiss. It is still customary for people to hit or clank their glasses to get the couple to kiss.

Superstitions

~ A gift of five almonds to wedding guests is a sign of wellbeing and wishes them: fertility, health, longevity, wealth, and happiness.

~ To ensure that the bride becomes friends with her mother-in-law, the mother-in-law should throw an old shoe over her shoulder.

~ Before the wedding, all the bridesmaids should write their names on the bottom of the bride's shoe. Whoever's name is still intact on the shoe after the wedding is the next one to marry.

~ If a woman falls down during the ceremony or reception, they will marry within the year.

~ An odd number of wedding guests is unlucky, contrary to this belief; in Asian cultures it is unlucky to have an even number of guests.

The Cake
Customs

The first wedding cakes began during the Roman Empire. A wheat cake was broken over the brides head as a symbol of the husbands' dominance over her and then was eaten for good luck and fertility.

In medieval England, guests brought their own breads or cakes to the wedding where they would pile them on a table and the higher the pile, the better luck and fertility the couple would have. The couple would then lean over the pile of cakes and try to kiss without knocking them over for good luck. In colonial New England they had "bride-cakes" that were served with cheese.

The current traditional three tier wedding cake developed within the last century and was inspired by the spire of the Saint Bride's Church in London, England. The cake topper of miniature bride and groom figurines became popular in America during the 1950's and represented the couple's togetherness. The cutting of the cake is the first symbol of the couple's unity together. Traditionally the man's hand is placed over the bride's as they slice the cake together, signifying he will take care of and protect her. Feeding the cake to one another is a symbol of their commitment to each other. In other cultures they feed each other different foods other than cake, like hot soup as a sign of trust.

Superstitions

~ The top layer of the cake is commonly kept frozen and eaten at the couple's one year anniversary. In England it is common for the top layer to be kept and used in the celebration of the christening of the couple's first child.

~ Every guest at the wedding reception is supposed to eat at least a bite of the cake to give the couple good wishes and good luck.

~ If a single woman sleeps with a piece of wedding cake under her pillow she will dream of her future husband.

~ The cake is traditionally white as a symbol of purity.

After the Wedding

Customs

The Threshold

The tradition where the groom carries the bride over the threshold has a few possible origins. The first theory is from when the bride was forced or kidnapped into the marriage and would not willingly go into her new home or the bedroom. The second is that it was ladylike to be hesitant to go into the bedroom and the husband would have to persuade or carry her into the room. The third theory is that it is considered bad luck for a bride to stumble or fall when she is entering her new home or the bedroom, so he would carry her to prevent bad luck.

Honeymoon

The use of the term honeymoon began because it described the first month of marriage as being the sweetest. It originated from Babylonian and Teutonic weddings where for one month (or one moon phase) after the marriage the newlyweds drank honey-wine, hence the name honey-moon. In the early 19th century the term honeymoon changed to when the couple would take vacation or holiday together. Some wealthy couples would take a "bridal tour" where they visited their family members that were unable to attend the wedding.

There also is another possible source of the honeymoon origin which is unpleasant to say the least. Some people believe that the honeymoon is another relic left over from bride kidnapping times where the bride would be forced into seclusion so her family could not find her. The groom's goal would be to impregnate his wife within the month of seclusion so her family could no longer disagree or protest their marriage because of the pregnancy.

Superstitions

~ The bride and groom should always use the main entrance to their home when entering the first time as a married couple for good luck.

~ The newlywed couple should borrow a coffee pot for the first three months of marriage, and then purchase one together.

~ It is unlucky to give away a wedding present even if it is not needed or wanted.

~ A marriage should never start with a used broom or frying pan; they should always have a new one.

~ Candles by the bed will keep away evil spirits.

~ For good luck, the first meal as a married couple should be made by the wife for both herself and her husband. They must not eat at a restaurant or family member's home.

~ To cure a husband of being ill tempered the wife should make soup from rain water collected from a rain shower on a Friday.

~ A bride must never sell her wedding dress after the wedding, it is very bad luck. It can be given away or borrowed, but never sold.

~ While on the honeymoon, the couple should be very careful to not break anything, especially a mirror which will bring a lot of bad luck.

~ An occasional fight during the honeymoon means the couple will have a long happy marriage.

Olde Time New England Weddings

Customs

In very early colonial settlements in New England, bride kidnapping was prevalent where young girls were carried off by men and forced into marriage. In western Massachusetts this was unfortunately common until Revolutionary times. In the Connecticut valley area, men that were not invited to the wedding would often invade the home where the ceremony was taking place and abduct the bride-to-be in the middle of the ceremony. They referred to this as "stealing the Mistress Bride." She then was hidden in another home or inn and was held for ransom.

One very strange disrespectful custom that woman did in New England was done to eliminate the debt or liability of her previous marriage to her new husband. It was called a "smock marriage" or "marriage in a shift" where a widowed woman with debt would marry her new husband nude. There are a few documented examples of these smock weddings, like the marriage of Major Moses Joy and Widow Hannah Ward in 1789 in Newfane Vermont. The ceremony took place in his home where she stood naked in the closet with the door shut which had a diamond shape cut out so she could hold his hand. Once the ceremony was done, she put on her wedding attire and emerged from the closet. Another example was the marriage of Widow Lovejoy in Westminster Vermont where she married her husband hidden in the chimney behind a curtain. In 1784 in New York an extremely unusual smock marriage took place on the gallows. The groom-to-be was condemned to death and was about to be executed, but was pardoned because of his marriage to a scantily clad woman at the gallows.

Traditional Colonial Weddings

The wedding ceremony in colonial New England was quite different than it is now. Invitations were commonly sent out only three days before the wedding. Many people considered it insulting if they received the invitation only one day in advance. Often the bridal couple would send out wedding gloves with the invitation as a gift to those invited. The gloves were actually an expensive gift and they were often gold-laced with fringes and rich gauntlets. It was also a colonial custom for guests to be invited to funerals with white gloves.

Marriage celebrations always had a rich thick drink called sack-posset. It was a concoction of boiled ale, eggs, and spices that was popular during Shakespearian times. Colonial Puritan's were not permitted to drink except on special occasions. When they were allowed to drink the sack-posset, they would read psalms before and after drinking from the Bay Psalm Book to make it a holy event. There was also a rich feast the night before the wedding, where it was customary for everyone to kiss and congratulate the bride. The only exception was that there were a few areas of New England where bride kissing was denounced. Dancing was another activity that was forbidden in colonial days from about 1651 until the mid-1700's, because they believed it often lead to fights and disorderly conduct, so this was not allowed even at weddings.

Even though the church was the foundation of everything during colonial times, the ceremony was not done by the minister. It was considered a civil union and was performed by a magistrate. The Sunday after the wedding the bride, groom, and wedding party would proceed to the church or meeting house, which was called "walking-out bride" or "coming out." They then would be prominently seated in the front of the meeting house for the Sunday sermon. Halfway through the service the minister would ask them to stand up and show off their wedding outfits to the rest of the congregation. Often the bride was honored by allowing her to choose that Sunday's sermon to be read by the minister.

Superstitions

~ Two spoons in one cup means a wedding will be held soon.

~ If you lose your garter or apron, you will lose your husband or he will be unfaithful.

~ If your apron becomes wet while doing the dishes, it means your husband will be a drunk.

~ To cure a drunken husband, hang your clothes wrong side out on a clothes line.

~ Tripping up the stairs means that you will not marry within the year.

~ If you easily build a fire it means your husband will be smart, if it's hard your husband will be lazy.

~ If you walk between two men on the street, it means you will marry both of them in your lifetime.

~ If you prick yourself with a needle while making a new garment, the first time you wear that garment you will be kissed.

~ If you step on a cigar stub you will marry the next man you meet.

~ If a girl gets the last piece of bread at the dinner table it means her husband will be handsome.

~ If you are handed a cup of tea, count the leaves of tea floating because that is the number of husbands you will have in your lifetime.

Miscellaneous

Customs

It was common for anything that made loud noises to be used at weddings. Things like horns, bells, whistles, cans, or even fireworks were used to ward off evil spirits to protect the newlyweds. Old cans and shoes were most common and were tied to the back of the vehicle, carriage, or wagon so as the couple drove away they would drag and make noise as they left.

Another old shoe custom started during Tudor times when guests would throw shoes at the bride and groom's carriage or car. If they hit the vehicle or carriage it would bring the thrower and the couple great luck. A gift of an old shoe was given to the groom by the bride's father as a symbol of handing over his daughter. The groom would then take the shoe and tap the bride's forehead to show his dominance over her.

Superstitions

~ If it is a full moon on the wedding day or a couple of days before it, it is considered good luck. If it is a couple of days past a full moon it is bad luck.

~ Two sisters should never share the same wedding day, they will both be cursed with horrible marriages.

~ If the car refuses to start on the way to the wedding, it means death is not far away.

~ If the bride sheds tears of happiness at her wedding, those will be the last tears she will shed during her marriage.

~ It is bad luck for the bride to read her marriage service before the wedding.

~ You should let a cat eat out of your left shoe one week before your wedding for good luck.

~ If a cat sneezes near the bride the day before or on her wedding day, it is good luck.

Wedding Terms

Bridal

The term bridal is actually from a British toasting tradition where the bride and groom would drink bride mead (honey wine) or "bride ale" which became the word bridal.

Groom

The word groom comes from the old English language word *byrd* which later developed into bride, and *guma* which meant young man. They combined the two words into *byrdguma* which described a young man searching for a bride. It later turned into bridegroom, and finally shortened to just groom.

Tie the Knot

This term is very old and originated in Celtic tradition from Handfasting ceremonies. It was an official "trial" marriage where the groom and bride would be married for one year and a day, or 13 moon cycles. If they lasted through this period of time, they either could handfast again, or officially get married. This type of ceremony was very simple where they held each other's wrists left to right, and right to left, forming an infinity symbol or knot (hence the term tying the knot). They then pledged devotion to each other in front of witnesses and shared a cup. This was common throughout England until the 1500's when marriage became government regulated.

Wedlock

This comes from the word *wedd* in the English language which means to pledge, and *lac* which means to carry out. They combined the two words into wedlock meaning to carrying out the pledge of devotion to one another in marriage.

References

Aiello, Dawn. (03/15/2007) Wedding Superstitions. Retrieved from http://www.thehistorybox.com

Bernstein, Harry. The Wedding Ring- History and Tradition. Retrieved from http://EzineArticles.com/?expert=Harry_Bernstein

Earle, Alice Morris. (April-June 1893) Old-Time Marriage Customs in New England. *Journal of American Folklore 6*, pages 97-102.

Ferland, Mallory. (03/20/2010) Ring Bearer Definition. Retrieved from http://www.ehow.com/about_6105300_ring-bearer-definition.html#ixzz1FBudRwz1

FlowerGirlInfo1. (10/31/2007) The Flower Girl Tradition in History. Retrieved from http://flowergirlinfo.net

Franklin, Rosalind. (2007) The Bride's Book of Wedding Superstitions. Diggory Press Inc., Goodyear Arizona.

Howard, Vicky (2006). Brides Inc.: American Weddings and the Business of Tradition. University of Pennsylvania Press, Philadelphia.

Price, A. (2001). Weddings. Great Britain: Creative publishing international.

Montemurro, Beth. "Origins of Bridal Showers and Bachelorette Parties". *Something Old, Something Bold*. Rutgers University Press. pp. 21–22. ISBN 0-8135-3811-4.

www.ingramcontent.com/pod-product-compliance
Lightning Source LLC
Chambersburg PA
CBHW071245280526
45788CB00004B/1595